D1484633

# MAKING THE NEW LAMB TAKE

# MAKING THE NEW LAMB TAKE

POEMS

## Gabriel Fried

Winner of the 2006 Kathryn A. Morton Prize in Poetry
Selected by Michael Ryan

Sarabande S Books
LOUISVILLE, KENTUCKY

Managing Editor
Sarabande Books, Inc.
2234 Dundee Road, Suite 200
Louisville, KY 40205

Library of Congress Cataloging-in-Publication Data

Fried, Gabriel, 1974 –
    Making the new lamb take : poems / by Gabriel Fried. — 1st ed.
        p.    cm.
    "Winner of the 2006 Kathryn A. Morton Prize in Poetry,
selected by Michael Ryan."
    ISBN-13: 978-1-932511-49-9 (pbk. : acid-free paper)
    ISBN-10: 1-932511-49-0 (pbk. : acid-free paper)
    I. Title.

    PS3606.R54M35 2007
    811'.6—dc22                              2006021541

Cover image: *Waverly, Pennsylvania*. Serigraph by Gretchen Dow
Simpson, provided courtesy of the artist.

Cover and text design by Charles Casey Martin
Manufactured in Canada
This book is printed on acid-free paper.
Sarabande Books is a nonprofit literary organization.

The Kentucky Arts Council, a state agency in the Commerce Cabinet,
provides operational support funding for Sarabande Books with state
tax dollars and federal funding from the National Endowment for the
Arts, which believes that a great nation deserves great art.

*For Alex*

# CONTENTS

# FOREWORD

I didn't know who wrote this book when I first read it. The poet turned out to be Gabriel Fried, thirty-one years old, who has a wife, a small son, and a job as an editor in New York. I knew this poet knew how sentences work, so his day job wasn't much of a surprise, but I thought he was older and I wouldn't have guessed he lived in New York City. The poems' small-town settings come from Fried's childhood home in an apple orchard eighty miles upstate, which probably informs their tone and certainly informs their texture. These settings also serve his intentions: the social group in which the speaker of these poems exists is cohesive (as in a small town), and it's perfect that this book begins with a poem in the first-person plural speaking about the odd effects on the community of a traveling fair that came and went. The "I" is subsumed in the "we." This poet's interest—unusual in a first book and even more unusual in a young man—is in other people as much as in himself, and in himself in relation to other people, both intimate (wife, son, family) and less intimate. What may be taken for reticence has its real source in a persistent need to understand the world in which he and other people live. In which *we* live. It's because of this focus—this seeking—that the poems gravitate toward myth and ritual, especially ritual social acts, such as in the extraordinary title poem, with its final twist of Psalm 23 ("He maketh me to lie down in green pastures": "we lead them into fields // and make them lie down.").

As in all good writing, Fried's style is an embodied expression of belief. It's a poetic style utterly transparent and unobstructing. I never think "Too many words!" or "What is he trying to say?" I am never bored and never confused. All the work is done for me on the page by language expertly rendered into sentences and lines and stanzas, but I partake of that work and enjoy its rewards. *Partake* in both the transitive and intransitive usages of that verb: to share in and to receive (as in a ritual). Fried's affecting attention to language—and the world of people and human feeling that language represents—determines the purpose of his style: its clarity is the clear lens of attention. And experiencing his attention enriches my own.

As engaging as Fried's sentences are as engines of movement, they rigorously serve meaning and music. His sentences are instruments of storytelling and, in conjunction with the line, instruments of song: the two ancient powers fundamental to poetry. We all tell hundreds of stories every day: stories are the way we reveal our inner lives to one another, by telling what's important or funny or strange, by saying what happened and what we feel. We literally couldn't live without them. Fried knows how to tell wondrous stories: they are shaped just right, perfectly balanced, sometimes beginning in the middle or not ending at the end: stories about pain and love, distress and consolation, about Cain and Abel, lambs and guard dogs, and the robin who repeatedly flies into his own reflection in a window glass with no chance "for seeing / what's beyond him." These stories are grounded in the sounds of words inextricable from their articulations, as both cause and effect. As Robert Frost said, "The ear does it. The ear is the only true writer and the only true reader." Fried's ear is a palpable presence at every nanosecond of these poems, at the brain-warp speed of language-processing. Internal rhymes and off-rhymes anchor and enrich the meanings of the sentences and their movements and the stories they tell, and in the few instances he uses end-rhyme and meter the forms are used essentially.

There are poets who publish early and conduct their education in public (like me) and there are poets who, young or not, are fully formed when they appear with their first books (like Whitman and Frost and Bishop). It's impossible for me to imagine poems more fully integrated or more fully realized than those in this book and it is heartening to me that these poems were written by someone young. That Gabriel Fried has the talent, skill, intelligence, and wisdom to have an exceptional future as a poet is unquestionable, but this first book of his already represents a mature accomplishment of the art.

—*Michael Ryan*

# MAKING THE NEW LAMB TAKE

# Traveling Fair

In the lot by the volunteer firehouse,
where boys burn their knees against
concrete learning to ride, it seems to grow
like night: from metal and dust, suddenly
solid, a small town's unexpected break
from smallness. Twice a year it comes to us—
shady, pagan, unconcerned with holy
days or school nights—and we let our young go
(we go ourselves), swept up like people
with a new machine. We're lifted above town,
beyond amusement, on the outstretched arms
of Zipper, Spin Out, Komikaze—more
risk than we invite in after sunset—
or slower, on the Ferris Wheel, smitten
by the fleshy glow the city gives the sky
far off, past all our woods and rivers.

These are moments of slack, of wander,
of full reversion to the old calm:
the feel of dough and pleasure of ascension.
There's been time since losing (the char

is off the pasture; now there is a stoplight)

and nothing we can hear cannot be

misheard as the whir of rides, of laughter,

or an unseasonable wind cutting

across town like a thru-road. By the time

we wake tomorrow, the fair will have been

razed, wax wrappers stranded in air

like trout when the creek goes dry in August.

Then, for days, the sense of something

different. No tree or rooftop high enough

to know for sure what lingers in our borders,

or who, under our charge, has left them.

# Hearing Child from a Deaf Household

I hear the silence they do.
Spherical and firm as buttons.
As if the mind, anesthetized, feels
just the tug of sound's stitching.
Splatter of dropped pot.
Dart of barking dog.

Sound is separate, surprising
as hail or remedy. At home,
I was a seismograph, an instructor
of muscle memory. There
I showed to close drawers softly.
But school was a hive that stings and will
not be shook off. There was the shock
of rubber on linoleum. Concussions
of blocks. Nothing I could think of—
no game I designed or found the quiet to
explain—made them stop.

Now, on Michigan back roads,
a flocculent snow whispers up

the windshield. The roads hold

secrets between them, snapped

back like branches or cold air slit

against an ear. Invisible as clotheslines

against this sky. Pounding as

a heart the whole world hears.

# The Mute of Hounds

Two dimensioned on the tightrope

made where hills intersect the sky,

the mute of hounds is on its horse again.


In August at dusk, the cavalier five of them—

brindled, black, and golden—

flit horizontal as if rabbits at the track.


The wind and hounds bound free up there,

having jumped the slopes

and blazed their way through bramble,


having hit that last hump

and punched free of trees.

Now, like banshees, they infiltrate the almost-dark.


They could be a trick of the setting sun

but see how the sun's too far declined.

See how they're not quite straight as rays.


See how the mute raises its throats in cries.

# Demigods

What else explains us
and our crystallized dominions?

One of us adventures through
the dark with confidence.

Another communes with water
birds—ducks flock around him

and speak, in turn, politely.
The third scarcely seems to touch

the humid clay when sculpting.
We have each prayed, separate

and sporadic, unannounced. We
have heard the rumors of a man

down the road whose arrival
no one noted and whose flowers

grow effortlessly out of season;

or the woman no one sees

but everyone gossips over,

who weaves chromatic scarves

from light on a weightless loom;

or other, half-remembered strangers.

What else explains how we hold

morning like a newspaper, wrestle

it, convince it of its atmosphere?

Who else can read in anagrams,

or recognize the quiet

dead boughs make before they fall?

Who else lays down these footprints,

vulpine in the unexpected snow?

# The Unnamed Season

The flowers have grown pointless and merely exquisite.

This is the moment I first believe

I might be thrilled by something dead.


Each crevice of this was mine,

each undiscovered trail and hillside.


Now I wander into town and make eyes,

leaving the screen door unlatched

as eggshells on the counter after breakfast.

# The New Garden

I return to find a prim new garden—
no bigger than a foyer.
It sits above true earth in planters,
a stoolpigeon shaken by the ankles
until the secret's out.

The old one, though, hid nothing.
It seemed to stretch to the horizon
beside the first experiments: A stream
dammed up. A cloud assuming shapes.
The boys rolling down a hill
growing closer to sky.

# Cloudburst

I've seen this storm since, miles off, it threw
itself in coughs against the Shawangunks, hazed
them up and down, then slugged its way
across their foothills, heading for home.

I've spent that time collecting cushions,
stowed rakes and mower underneath the porch.
I've kept one eye directed at the sky,
bracing for the storm in its approach.

Inclemency weighs, saturate, around
my face. Above, few strips of blue survive.
Air cools. The drenching of the dale below
the road rolls through itself like links of chain.

Some tulips purse nearby with hunch of rain.
A sparrow shutters in its lilac bush.
At once, the road's loose dust erupts, and just
as I've heard it said, the skies open up.

# Dollhouse

In it is spoken a perfect, sanded Dutchman's English
which, like the house itself, leaves clear
one wall, intangible—is sheer.

What built it—little hands and one small lack
of wood—took time to think of light,
had plans to put down roots—had sight.

Each room, the length of a bit of crust, is open
in back like an apron. Each stair
holds peril on one side—the air.

A desk, a thimble stove, and four whittled chairs
have backboards pressed against the wall.
A little thing takes little push—to fall.

# Making the New Lamb Take

The skin is only perfume now.
It won't take seed and grow: cells

clot like sand, the vellus curling
from both ends in tendrils.

We have lifted it—careful—off,
waiting for a breeze to taper until air

is no enemy, dried sheets tugging
down the line. Underneath is flesh

too fresh for day, like eyes that spend
the hours mining in dream or lamplight.

Working there, while at it, we hear
the mourning ewe from the bluish fields

she wanders—a harbormaster
who has ruined single-mindedness.

And though it doesn't do one stitch
of good, we think of her.


We cannot tell her it is not her doing,
knowing how our own don't always live,


or won't live well.
We cannot lie, even in our lingual tongue,


which must make muddled sense
to her, at best. (One stray sound


among many sticks, then ticks off
into the chasm.)


Instead, we bind the fleece
to the back of another: young, just


seeing, of a more prosperous mother
who's tired from all the mouths at her.


We tie the flapping ankles tight
with hemp, then hood the head over,

both mouths now silenced.

This disguise was never meant


for sight, so we guide them,

the old aroma warming underneath,


leash taut with mute resistance.

They say the ewe will come to love


him after weeks; I have my doubts.

But underneath the clouds—like clouds


themselves, led by contrary winds—

we lead them into fields


and make them lie down.

# Nursery

Fall hasn't been for long, yet
already I miss summer's promise:
Ever endless days are past

where if I drew a chart
of what I've done, it would
be what I hadn't quite.

I know the shape of what remains—
kicking up August dust,
evoking waxen words

that won't be touched—
a gourd-sized box, implying
what's inside it.

# Mid-Fall

I'm back and forth
on this back-and-forth
bus enough to think,

I'll take it back,
what I said about
falling in love. Can't I

just rake it in,
stuff it under my shirt,
itching like a martyr

scarecrow who
won't move his arms
to let his guts out?

I won't spill myself
like stringy sap without
a round-trip ticket

to take it back

like a tourist checking out

foliage as days give way,


the clock falls back,

trees bare themselves,

and cover leaves me.

# The Places We Knew
# Not to Go as Children

The places we knew not to go as children
we went anyway. Something in the jag
and shimmer of them herded us. Something
in their surfaces enchanted us. Something
seeming sticky. The bog that bores into
the orchard like decay into a tooth glistens
like a ball field with algae. We walk on
floorboards in the hayloft, daring loosened
planks to flip us down to cement floors.
We return to the troubling shack out
in the woods, to its mattress and paddle.
We listen to the murmurs of the unmarked
well, shining like a wound amid the field,
echoing, *It is safe, it is safe as houses.*

# The Hole

Beyond the house, on the edge of forest,
there is digging. Incredibly, men work

at it in daylight, as if they started
it or understand its purpose. I was

not there, but I remember the night, moon
rising above a hill, when a sound crept

among other sounds like something wanting
in quietly—and for no known reason.

There was no shovel, and no man's breathing.
It didn't dig like man, with a kerchief;

there was no lamp half-full of kerosene
or headlights aimed anxiously at darkness.

Yet man was there, a part of the rumor
no one remembers. A part of him was

buried deep, or in need of burial,

and so he joined in, trusting and aligned


with the first friendly face who spoke a word

or two of his language. This is how


a hole grows: bigger or smaller, banking

on muscle memory and willingness.


Neighbors lend tools, or pull on garden gloves

themselves, planting spades in heavy earth.


None know what for. Some assume it's plumbing.

Others simply love the slap a shovel


makes and need no explanation. They know

they'll dig until the moon again begins


its climb; until they knock against a lid

or pat one down—when something is exposed,


or nothing is.

# To Zita, Patron Saint of Lost Keys

At once, it seems that all is latched,

and I feel like the hunter feels, caught

in his own bear-trap, held in the clasp

of winter: alone, atonal, birds bored

by my intermittent efforts.


                      Why has your god left

me here in openness? Tell him I will

unlock his arks and boxes, and light

the incense he has left there. (Though

if his errands are so urgent he should

surely leave a set with someone less

fraught by flightiness.) Tell him

I will cross into whatever city-state

that jilts him to deliver ultimatums

to aldermen behind closed doors.

Tell him I will circulate his name

at parties, and underline important

passages. Tell him I will use specific

candelabras and dishware if only

I can unlock the cupboard. I will

imagine other things dissolving on

my tongue if the pantry door unfastens,

and I will eat what and when he says,

though it is not my craving. Tell him

the milk will soon spoil and the cows

have not wronged him; or of the urgency

of mortal errands. (They keep us from

dumb ruin.) Or tell him—for I fret

beyond fear of shame—the children

have stopped wailing too suddenly,

the windows (double-paned, too thick)

fogged over from their recent breath.

# Guard Dog

It takes this porch to make her mythic

to herself—this square of rail and floorboard.

From here she sees the dense red clay. Beyond

the marshes, the tides commit themselves to borders.

From this she understands the meaning

of property and sightline. She feels at last

the well of rumbling, and lets the howls gallop

up her throat at any motion from the edges,

at any shadow that, without a coin, would pass her.

# Demeter, after

Each farmer loses something of the harvest;
each has planted rows too near the forest.

I've lost myself in losing her.
The torch is cast aside and smolders.

I return now, after years, to work the earth
as one returns to sex: Not to sow. To rehearse.

To feel the cold dirt pressed against the wrist.

# White Dwarf Star

An autumn unlike others.
The heat absorbed in summer

lost. Hands clumsy, gloves misplaced.
Nothing smells of anything but slate.

The galaxy kicks about, local as dust
shook up behind a county bus:

an unclenching of personal mass,
released by a tired-out watch clasp.

Nothing to resist, no one to give in to.
Grass yellowed. Leaves, let loose, marooned.

# Processional

The dead come clean and curious,
without the pulse the living have

to argue. Impeccable in washed-out
seersucker, smelling of peppercorns

and copper, they traipse their hems
through grass they cut themselves,

along the lawns where they spend days.
They almost walk with purpose

toward the tent-fold, soft as bakers
or flightless birds who've known no predator.

But nothing is unanswered anymore.
They each have just the one question, a hair

in their peripheral vision, barely noticed
underneath the pale, flat sun that has now risen,

that no one noticed set. Inside the tent,

the patient dead all find their seats and wait.

# The Insomniacs' Afterlife

Unprepared for the exotic stillness

elsewhere capturing their bodies, their souls

stand separate, muscular and splintered

as phone poles stacked with homemade signs

at distant crossroads. Before them, the fields

are kind and uncomplicated. Others

stroll about them freely, kites unknotted

from the branches in October—let loose

and gliding with deserved mobility.


The insomniacs, though, are rooted in place,

each one bearing the expression

of the just-discovered-uttering. The embedded

world moves past in all directions—like night can

sometimes pass a lamp-lit window undetected.

# In Search of Ba & Ka

I am unhappy with the diphthonged words for soul

and aura. The wild boar cavort

through the unpeopled desert dawn.

In an hour, the day will be ablaze,

sweat an inevitable, bodily solution

to the pyramid of sun compressing us.


Why have I come?

To know the unadulterated passions?

Smogless, untreated with pills, art, or jargon?

Was it merely to know that we can

never hide within our shadows?

By noon, we stand revealed above them,


golf carts passing in the place of boar—

boxy, hairless, asyllabic

as the mission bells that linger all day.

It will be dusk before it's cool

enough to walk with infants alongside

the riverbed, their fat hands browning

in the sun, their soft mouths poised

to part with their first consonantal sounds.

# Family Gathering

No one here has ever seen the desert
or the meadows of the afterlife.

I still love weddings (I try to make it
home for those), but I feel unwelcome

at funerals. I do not cause their deaths,
of course; but by now I must admit

that I do not improve their living.
For this, I am mistrusted, as grazing

herds mistrust the crows on either side
of carnage. In time, I tell myself,

I will detach from my own stillness,
become a witness of my own restraint.

For now, I shake the seething
off me like a dog shakes off pond water,

or a boy waggles off grain as he emerges

like a migrant from the fields.

# Burial

At eight, he's too young to fill a grave,

but the grown-ups' efforts were half-hearted.


So he stands above the hole—just two feet

long, but deeper—and goes at it,


the shovel above him, standing him up.

He swings like a tiny back-hoe,


getting just a mug of dirt each time.

This hole was built to suit him, though,


and after several strokes, he's at full steam.

It's not that no one wants to stop him:


Even the gravediggers watch him

as he seems to grow a little short with time.


He barely blinks, and with each pitch

the left pinch of his lips caves twice:

once with the rip of shovel in earth,

once when the dirt smacks the wooden lid.


In moments, he's become master

of driving the shovel in with his heel,


of pulling it back mid-fling to let the dirt fall.

It's filling now, the grave, overflowing,


so he gives a final heave and pats it down.

Then he stands the shovel up, and looks beyond us.


He's got work to do, it's sad work, and he knows it.

# The Scarecrow Fair

They struggle like men trying to be proud

before the sea. From a distance,

it's hard to tell if they are soulless,

or if something huddles up inside

like a hutch of rabbits; and up close,

it's painful how their posture

will not please them or pull them

far enough from itch to matter.


On a middle ground, though—a raise

that neither praises nor degrades them—

we can see that they were born

content (maybe in a caul of darkness,

a sharp nest of shapelessness) not knowing

who they were or what their danger is.


Some may accuse them of morbidity,

of waiting for the ambulance to form

from the wind's high pitch through dunes.

But their job, if it can be named, is reminding

us we each grew up in one sort of countryside,

among decomposition and the high grasses:

We are, all of us, a product of our own

pre-industry, a tool-less time

when voices weren't heard rasping behind

air, and our own hands filled our gloves.

We each saw as individuals the fox steal

onto the trail. We memorized that

exact topography, the one we thought

we'd come back to in years to come:

the trail cutting clear through the acreage

and into farms abutting like dialects,

soil slightly different, figures rearranged.


Roots were not as ruthless then.

We did not hate them so for wanting us

kept close or all at once betraying us

to an ungrounded sky.

# The Scarecrow Makers

I.

I've promised I'll find other uses
for my hands.

I'll ignore the purposeful
machine monthly going

through its motions like fire
drills or children

climbing off and on buses.
Instead I'm given

objects to keep
busy, ones that won't make me

reach or beckon: thimble,
sextant, putty, loose

leaf, felt. Each forms its own kind
of trouble, like puns I used

to make, back when I could make
more than one sense of things.


## II.


Midday. Sun slops.
I shove hay
into hoods and gloves.
It's like having fun
with guts.


Once people
let me kill swine—
just one summer's
worth of slaughter.


Now they sic
reaping on me,
scared of what they made

of my last stabs

at it.


They don't know nothing

in my hands will end

up looking

how they like.


Stick sweat-close.

I'll remind you

of the spoke-less shape.


You remind me when

to scratch the love-rash

from skin.


III.


I fear we build

what scares us off

our perch. Heads

of daisy, tinsel:

they seemed so

pretty in our eyes,

even out of light.


At first, they were.


But gathering grew

rounder, corners less

roomy. The nest began

to creak like organs

punctured in tandem

at the laying out

of some strange field.


Hollowness begins

to fill with something

slightly heavy. Ill winds

blow us up, and force us,

fitful, down.

# Alone Enough

The ants, hill razed, are breaking camp,

the washed-out flowerbed still damp.


The moon, once flawless and ample

as a cufflink, sidles from the disrupted puddle.


Elsewhere, the tired spider begins its web again,

and the dormice redig their den.


Even farmers roll their keepsakes into packs,

their seeds dug up, their green things sacked.


Milkweeds, torn from pods, disperse in tufts.

I cannot leave well alone enough.

# Disinterment

For years I've waited in the dirt for God—
my patience limitless and firm
from practice. From within my perfect pose,
I have designed the perfect form
for heaven. In it, we are both muse
and maker, each of us a portion
of an unframed sea alive with motion.
We draw back curtain after curtain,
learning the world as newborns must
before the storm: Some shapes. A ripple.
A melody, instantly embedded.
We float among the reeds below the highway,
nape and ankles gripped from underneath,
a glacier glinting in moonlight—
its movement undetectable and onward.
We are clotted full of time as photographs
will be—praiseworthy and changing
everything—like little pelt-proud creatures,
unaware that soon the metal scrape above
our den will menace us with vanity and vision.

# Abel, after

It is seldom told, less often written—


I wake as a lamb in my brother's flock.
Newborn, I cannot stand, and long for milk
so wholly I begin at once to knell
with a sound that shocks my humanness.


In the moments before the breast has come,
I sense myself, but primal. Want, trust, lung:
this is the lifetime I've run from—seconds
long, then gone. I drink and, numb, remember.


My brother clutches something in his fist.
He is a shepherd now, spurned by the earth,
and yet a father: his children spill forth,
milkweed about fields once lined by bald seeds.


In no time, I grow woolen. The flock dollops
up the landscape like a tract of gravestones.
The other sheep, base and dumb as schoolyard
thugs or hack ventriloquists, call him *Mark*.

He comes to them by daylight, open hand

grazing each fleece he passes, giving

as a wet nurse, and as impermanent.

They bleat at him, resentful and longing


for some deep (or even violent) tug

that lasts them. I remember offerings

to a new god: winds dismissed my carnal

smoke in gusts; what my brother offered stayed,


gems in heavenly earth. O, to see them

there in twilight! Beets and peppers plumper

than pearls—unacceptable and blessed.

His crop was hoarded by and for the world.


Now, new moons (mother's eye shut above),

the old knife flecks in star—more trowel than blade,

its hilt held flat against his palm.

His sandals pad like the rote of the sea.


How is it he finds me in the darkness?

I hide from him to test him, as always

his way to me like woven, edgeless birth.

Here is where love is fiercest: anywhere

with roots. Even this barren plain has them.

They pin the night around us like a tent,

too small, in which we breathe each other's breath,

close enough to be a candle's oval heat.


Gently, he takes the skin below my jaw

with his free hand. He bunches it in folds

so we can feel my beat as if it's ours,

as if we didn't know what hones this life.


My brother touches me; he's touched me twice.

# Noah's Dove

People rough you up,

then move on. They have

their orders, believe

in them, or need to

want to. I have seen this.

I have flown

in routes I did not choose,

gathering

twigs and branches.

I have found myself

above an endless water

I knew I shouldn't drink,

and have found sad pleasure

in the chores before me,

though I disappoint

myself fulfilling others'
missions; but they praise
my cleverness, give me

seeds I've been eying.
For this, I know I squander
life. I peck the ground

in stupid places, deliver
messages I care nothing
for. Of course I have

thought of change,
of flying off and leaving
their eyes straining.

I sense I know the way
to gems and soft heather,
to perfect houses that fit

me with a halo's safety.
I have my own missions,
and would launch them,

*have* launched them

each time out, falsely

assenting to some other errand,


only to remember—the ship

behind me, the feeling

that the earth protrudes


ahead—that I have been man-

handled and my mother

will never love me.

# Cain

Then I stood and saw the bur of clotting earth. Red
as an umbilicus. Shredding. Bricky. Slick. Things

that do not stay together in the new logic—too bright
for the silence I've invented.

I am not the first to know a recent past, to be clutched
by forceps in the dark:

See the bruises on my mother's thighs.
See my father's wrists and knuckles,

scraped on the inevitable
stones and rust that keep him from arable soil.

Look what I've done with their flaw: I've made it rash,
infection, epidemic. They thought that they rebelled

with their hashish, their banned books and agnosticism.
But anyone can ride a motorcycle.

I've marked my brow

by wiping it clean with the back of my hand.

# Running from the Gods

They keep coming, puppies grown too big

for games of tear, tear, kill, kill—

nails too thick to trim,

haunches strong as a drawbridge.

Why did we ever take them in?

Now they link our scent

with comfort and roughhouse.

They hunt through the rubble

of a ruined city, finding shreds of denim

on the asphalt where we've fallen.

We succumbed to thinking

they would never turn on us,

though we'd seen the dribbled

juices on their chins as they basked,

too content, in the autumn sun.

And they buried their noses into us

so deeply we felt almost prepubescent,

large yet shy from such thick interest.

How did we ignore the signs

of their increasing hunger?

Remember, we attempted to dismiss

what others told us as mere rumor.

What were we so proud of

that we huddle now across

county lines, covered in straw

behind the faded paint

of an old barn door?

What did we want so badly

we felt we had to pray?

# Dora's Third Dream

The third dream I tell no one:


A great rug fills an empty room.

Sun bakes through a window high above

like something's meant to grow here.

Outside, the ocean rubs unnoticed on

the kneecaps of the house, near a girl's

skirt laid out too long on the rocks to dry.

Now it's stiff with sand and salt.


The tide approaches. A carriage comes

around the bend, dark and blistered

like the inside of a sheath. There is an urge

to exit through a door, a pungent swelling.


The rug is thick, the room just painted, I am hot as pitch.

# Eurydice

Through the toxic atmosphere,

       beneath the neon light of a pistachio moon,

             I see my lover's perfect, unkempt

hair, which ends in shapely scalpels


       at the nape of his immortal neck.

       I want to take him in my mouth, hold him

             by that nape as if he were a whelp; stand guard

around the case for that unrivaled instrument—his throat.


       He sings softly as he walks ahead of me

       (though not quietly) about the songs he'll sing

             to me come morning: something for the surfers

on the Gulf of Enez; a verse describing


clothing I'd folded on the arm of a chair;

       a melody he's writing for the nymphettes

             who are hired to protect the Siphinos swans.

His voice seems disembodied, in stereo

from speakers on the walls that I can't see.

Then again, it always *seems* apocryphal,

        such euphony routed through so delicate an oriface.

Sometimes, when I embrace him, his breath


        transports an inadvertent spasm of song,

    which plays my vocal cords like a loon's

        and rings my knees like sacks of dimes.

Even here, back bent on the Hell path,


where daydreams seem, at best, untenable,

    an ecstasy accrues inside me, the approaching

        of a tiny train; waves cresting,

nonetheless, at low tide.


    How slippery the moss is underfoot,

    as are the whetted hand-holds I grope for.

        I find my frock bogged down, dank,

adhering to my thighs as oil does


        to an epidermis of roadside puddle.

    It's been so long since I sat among the ducks,

I realize now. I strain to imagine how they shimmy

as they make straight for a stalk or crouton;


how they snap at their own reflections,

      tail feathers turned upwards like talismans to sky.

      I've imitated them—exceded them, even—

by plunging down to murkiness.


      Don't think that you emerge unchanged.

      I came in coy, and now return dangerously

          unmindful. I know this even as I am

distracted by the dappling of a foreign sky,


            one which strobes about me so I don't know

      where or what I mean. Delighted, I need only

         wander off the path a bit to place myself

directly underneath its central star, to make myself


chief apothegm of its imperfect sphere.

      And how the moss now feels like glue, like velvet!

      So I spin in place, watching mallards migrate

through my vortex, seasons suddenly set in motion.

Unenchanted, you can't name every season.

Spring, Goblet, Dry Wall—these are the first three,

        the only ones I can as yet pronouce.

They're longer than you'd think, though still


              of different lengths each time around. You measure

          them

    by water's thickness in a hilltop lake:

        The seasons turn in the reflection, along with faces

recognizable as not your own.


If you ignore most everything, it seems

    as if it couldn't be coincidence, what you see reflected.

        Right now I can see mallards winging southward;

below, an ashen silhouette, and I am turning.

# Orpheus, after

The sand scorches
the tendons
of my perforated neck
as all sounds scorch
my eardrums dumb.
My tongue flops like cod.
The blood-let persists,
unending.

How human,
this cornucopia,
this overspilling;
and yet, how like the sun,
a ball let loose
and held to earth
by its own
intangible fibers.

# Diurnal

Some days, there is a lake's wholeness.
No one organ wanders off or worries.


Other days, the stack of sorted papers
topples into uncommitted piles.


That the dog won't play is enough
to cause a heart to break


away and hide in one of its four chambers.

# The Robin

He comes in early spring.
I hear the smack of him
against the window by the lilac bush
and armoire as he throws himself
at his reflection with a single-minded
violence and a certain heavy music.
Three years now he's been here
in the weeks before the air is warm
enough to raise the storm panes.
By now he's made a thousand notches
in the glass, scars where he has struck
himself for hours at a time, until he's forced
to rest across the road in bramble.
I know he thinks it is another bird
he sees, rushing from within
the window's shady versions—
but another bird like him,
exactly: the swollen ochre chest,
the rounded head a sallet.
He continues when I stand there
at the sill, his image flying from me

like the spirit of a dead man.

As a man, I do not scare him, even

if I scare myself sometimes—before

the armoire mirror, making faces.

He can't see past the symmetry

he makes with each collision,

the two of him so square with trying

to get *out* and *at* and *in* that they impede

what chance he has for seeing

what's beyond him: Three blue eggs

and soil turned to something giving.

# The Retrieval

It's like with dreams on waking: the deads' message toothless
and broken, the path to a sublime topography hidden; a memory

of freight trains trudging the old tracks impossible, the bridge
they led to up in flames a month before my birth and left there,

a body kept too long above the small sharp mouths
of a larderless December. The clear notion loses shape.

Leaves yellow and crumble, shedding sense
and syntax, living on only as the formless scraps of winter.

But even in winter there's ignition, spleens seeping
in the cracks of hard soil. As it sets, the sun makes a cold

torch with the mountaintop tower the painters all omit.
It blossoms through the sky before it dwindles

to a candle, carried westward, a small fire being
brought back down from the mystery of the mountain.

It's carried slow at first for fear of its own wind, then faster

as the wood or wax that bears it burns away, threatening to


disappear before it can transform the huddled homes down

in the valley, whose residents can barely see the coming night.

# The Thaw

Gone are the seasons of bruise and shatter.

In their place, a brave flesh gathers.

Brave and feeling as fir trees in a forest.


One day we will speak about the darkness—

when you are older and I am old.

We, too, may have to speak about the cold


of where we've been. Of the separate

sounds we woke to, our breath apparent:

the chisel, the lone fox scuffling for morsels


on a meadow so long frozen it's demoralized

the sun. But for now we bask within the spark

we've made. The flick that thawed the visible heart.

# In Utero

They call it kicking,
but tonight I listen closely,
my ear pressed tight
against the swell
of belly, and I hear it:
He is building something
in there. Something solid,
with what tools he has.
And how his elbow
(not foot) lashes—
I did that as a boy, behind
the house: little saw strokes
and two-handed hammer taps.
I built benches to sit on—
rough, tiny, barely shaped.
But sturdy, set down right
within the shade of eaves
I made them in. Where would I
have put them but where
the grass is cool and nothing
hadn't been how I conceived of it?

The future small and crucial,

pumping blood into its own

most distant capillaries,

needing nothing but its own

two legs to stand on.

# The Circumcision

Days after that first hurt (when he was first

not with us and we first awaited his return),


his foreskin crept back up him like evening

creeps: unnoticed and then all at once upon its bit


of scenery. Though what should we have hoped

to find beneath the bloody gauze but what will be


his private self recovered? What scars

there are concealed until the sun goes down,


and one by one they permeate his night like stars—

# Last Day of the Pantheon

Who would have thought that after years

of fruitfulness the trees would go barren

as mules, hollow out, and fall, almost

all at once, field after field, one summer?

First, though, the apples went funny:

mackintosh and jonathans like rocks

boys split unlovingly with bats.

Had they been human, we'd have checked

the water and soil. (We won't tolerate

a bad crop of our own kind.) But maybe

we were run too ragged by wounding,

or the old porch needed painting. One way

or another, we didn't care enough,

or there was too much to care for;

our prayers weren't heard, or were

misheard; or we went to pray but couldn't—

not here, with these trees, this inscrutable

landscape. How could we, from such a lack

of distance, bent over a hive or stump?


This was before your time. Now a quince bush

no one planted starts to bear fruit that's fat

as toddlers. Its singularity is

one sort of answer: the sun insists on

rising, the well is not nearly empty,

and something modest succeeds in our midst.

The quinces are perfect. We could stay

with them, one ancient culture ceding

to the next, taking on old rituals, dutifully

carried forth like baskets to the river.

But in this morning's paper, I read

about the stars, and how they are saying

they've discovered some new form of matter.

# First Day of a New Myth

This morning feels no different. But
last night the dreams subsided: dead women

stopped weaving. Sheets didn't curdle
around me, freeing a slick mattress.

Still, something must have crawled through.
A tabby or beetle. The door is cracked,

there is an airless draft, though the weather
vane shuffles, aimless.

There are no other omens. Steam still
shoots through the kettle, and the kitchen

window rattles in the pane when the mail
truck hits the pothole.

The dog does her usual business, whining
at the flue ghosts, baying

at the naval clock's chimes. It's not

as if the fourth step's stopped squeaking,


or the stain on the ceiling below

the tub has suddenly vanished. Today,


as on other days, I know someone will

stumble quick upon a snake, and I will


have to wonder what will happen

once I've cleared my throat.

# Pandora's Box

Whatever's written of it, it must be wooden—
lacquered, perhaps, but simple. Hinged,
but not intricate. Fundamental. Fitting.
It would be something we find as children—

in a house, maybe ours, maybe somewhere
in our parent's living room or an uncle's
drawer. Someplace we could linger, feel
as if we owned it, figure how to work it.

Perhaps it has some other function,
something neither clever nor childish:
a case for snuff or matches, storing tiles.
Perhaps it is a box for cards, dense enough

to hold in two hands—painted symbols
for each suit like pressed leaves on top—
that opens when we take both thumbs
and push them wholly on the heart.

# Notes and Dedications

In "The Mute of Hounds," *mute* is an archaic synonym for *pack* (as in, pack of hounds).

"In Search of Ba & Ka" refers to two spiritual notions of ancient Egypt: In simple terms, the ba was considered to be a person's non-corporeal essence, while the ka was his or her life force.

"Disinterment" is based on the life, death, and poetry of Pre-Raphaelite muse Elizabeth Siddal (1829–1862). Siddal was disinterred by Dante Gabriel Rossetti, her husband, who wished to retrieve the sole manuscript of his poems, which he had buried with her in his grief at the time of her death. I am grateful to Carolyn Williams for introducing me to Siddal's poems.

"Dora's Third Dream" is written after Sigmund Freud's *Dora: An Analysis of a Case of Hysteria*.

\*

"Hearing Child from a Deaf Household" is for Nicole Dogwill.

"The Insomniacs' Afterlife" is for Lisa Russ Spaar.

"Burial" is for Isaac Rosen.

"The Thaw" is for Archer Fried-Socarides.

# ACKNOWLEDGMENTS

Thanks to the editors of the following journals in which the following poems first appeared, sometimes in previous versions or with different titles:

| | |
|---|---|
| *American Literary Review* | "Abel, after" |
| *American Poetry Review* | "Making the New Lamb Take" |
| | "Scarecrow Fair" |
| | "Traveling Fair" |
| *The American Scholar* | "Diurnal" |
| *Barrow Street* | "The Insomniacs' Afterlife" |
| *Drunken Boat* | "The Hole" |
| | "Hearing Child from a Deaf Household" |
| *The Gettysburg Review* | "Pandora's Box" |
| *The Great River Review* | "Alone Enough" |
| | "Demigods" |
| | "Mid-Fall" |
| | "White Dwarf Star" |
| *The Paris Review* | "Eurydice" |
| | "Orpheus, after" |
| *Prairie Schooner* | "Cloudburst" |
| *Southeast Review* | "Dollhouse" |
| | "Nursery" |

For their essential support of this collection, I am forever grateful to a handful of wonderful people, including the stalwart staff of Sarabande Books, led by Sarah Gorham; Robert Farnsworth and Richard Howard, two poets whose generosity, insight, and friendship have been central to my life and to my writing; Lisa Russ Spaar, night goddess; and, of course, Michael Ryan.

Thanks, too, and love to my father, who shared such wonderful stories from the beginning; and to my mother, who imparted a deep connection to the physical earth that is, to me, a central part of these poems.

Lastly, I want to convey what can only be an inadequate expression of love, gratitude, and devotion to Alexandra Socarides, for whom this book was written and whose contributions to it and its author are too numerous and profound to name. *We end in joy.*

# THE AUTHOR

Gabriel Fried grew up in upstate New York. His poems have appeared in a number of journals, including *The American Scholar*, *Drunken Boat*, *The Gettysburg Review*, *The Great River Review*, and *The Paris Review*. He lives in New York City, where he edits the poetry series at Persea Books.

79